Collateral Damage: Misogyny, Misinformation, and Public Health

The Intersections of Misogyny, Misinformation, and Decline

Barbara Ann Johnson

Chapter 1: Collateral Damage

Summary: This chapter introduces the foundation of the book, presenting the interconnected themes of health risks, misinformation, misogyny, and societal shifts. It sets the stage by discussing the prevalence of misinformation and its impact on public health, particularly regarding high-risk behaviors and their unspoken consequences.

The night sky was clear, yet the city hummed with an unseen tension. Beneath the glow of streetlights, truths remained buried, silenced by layers of stigma, misinformation, and willful ignorance. Collateral damage—the term echoed in headlines and whispers alike. It was the price paid not just by individuals but by entire communities, their lives shaped and reshaped by forces few dared to confront.

For decades, public health campaigns had focused their spotlight on the importance of awareness and prevention. Yet, lurking beneath these efforts was an unspoken reality: the systemic failure to address the root causes of rising health crises. Conversations were drowned in political correctness or distorted by narratives designed to deflect responsibility. The real risks, the real stories, were hidden in plain sight.

A Crisis of Silence

Consider the statistics: In the United States, 67% of new HIV diagnoses are among gay and bisexual men, a staggering number for a group often reported to comprise only 5–7% of the population. Anal sex, recognized as the riskiest type of sexual activity for HIV transmission, rarely garners the level of public discourse its significance demands. This disconnect—between the scale of the issue and society's willingness to address it—was not merely accidental; it was engineered.

"It's misinformation," one epidemiologist stated during a quiet moment at a health conference. "We're inundated with half-truths designed to preserve comfort, not confront reality." Comfort, it seemed, had become the enemy of progress. Conversations about health risks were sanitized,

stripped of nuance, and reassembled as palatable soundbites. But the consequences of this approach could not be ignored.

Misinformation extended beyond health data. Cultural narratives downplayed risks and romanticized lifestyles without acknowledging their complexities. Advocacy groups, in their push for equality, sometimes skirted the uncomfortable truths of public health. And within this silence, a shadow grew—of mistrust, misunderstanding, and mounting harm.

The Gender Divide

Misogyny flourished in unexpected places, including communities that had themselves faced marginalization. For years, women had been silent casualties in the struggle for visibility and validation. They bore the brunt of societal hypocrisy, often exposed to health risks by partners who lived double lives.

Infected indirectly—through the whispered secrets of a male lover and his hidden male companion—these women found themselves victims of betrayal and a public health system that failed to address their plight. The Centers for Disease Control and Prevention (CDC) reported heterosexual transmission as a leading cause of HIV infections among women. But these numbers were more than statistics; they were stories of lives forever altered.

"The stigma is unbearable," one woman shared during an interview. "You're judged for something you didn't choose, something you didn't even know was happening."

But misogyny extended beyond health. It lurked in cultural narratives, where femininity was mocked or dismissed, even within LGBTQ+ communities. Articles like *The Advocate*'s "15 Signs You're a Gay Misogynist" and *Vice*'s exposés revealed a harsh reality: disdain for women, even among gay men, was not uncommon. The disdain was subtle but pervasive, manifesting in language, actions, and the exclusion of women from spaces meant to celebrate diversity.

A Mental Health Crisis Unacknowledged

At the heart of these issues lay an often-ignored truth: the role of mental health. Conditions like pica, linked to underlying psychological disorders, served as a stark reminder of how untreated mental illness could influence behaviors and decisions. Yet, discussions of mental health often remained siloed, disconnected from broader conversations about public health and societal dynamics.

Untreated psychological conditions didn't just impact individuals—they rippled outward, influencing relationships, communities, and cultural norms. And within these ripples, misinformation found fertile ground.

The consequences of inaction were clear: rising infection rates, fractured trust between communities, and a growing divide between the narratives society upheld and the realities people lived. The silence surrounding health risks, misogyny, and mental health wasn't just ignorance—it was complicity.

As the city continued to hum, its lights casting long shadows on quiet streets, the question remained: How long could these truths remain hidden? And what would it take to confront them, openly and honestly?

Chapter 2: The Roots of Misinformation

Summary: This chapter delves into how misinformation about health risks, societal dynamics, and cultural stigmas emerged and persisted. It examines the role of advocacy, media, and societal norms in shaping narratives that often obscure uncomfortable truths, emphasizing how these misrepresentations have contributed to public health crises and reinforced systemic misogyny.

The war on truth is rarely fought with overt lies. Instead, it is waged through omission, half-truths, and carefully curated narratives. For decades, misinformation has shaped societal understanding of health risks, intimacy, and the cultural dynamics of marginalized communities. Far from benign, this misdirection has left a trail of broken systems, fractured trust, and unaddressed harm.

At the heart of this phenomenon lies a paradox: the push for equality and acceptance has, at times, collided with the need for transparency about the health risks associated with certain behaviors. Conversations meant to promote visibility and inclusion have often avoided the darker realities lurking beneath the surface. And in this silence, myths flourish.

The Rise of Sanitized Narratives

In the late 20th century, public health campaigns shifted from warning to reassuring. The tone of these messages changed, not out of malice, but in response to a growing awareness of the stigma surrounding marginalized groups. Fear-based narratives gave way to a more palatable approach—one that prioritized inclusion over clarity.

Take, for example, the dialogue around HIV and AIDS. Early campaigns, which focused on the dangers of unprotected sex, often ignored the complex social and behavioral factors contributing to the crisis. As advocacy for LGBTQ+ rights grew louder, public health efforts softened their messaging to avoid further stigmatizing gay and bisexual men. While this was a well-meaning attempt to combat discrimination, it left critical gaps in education about the risks of anal sex, the rising rates of HIV among certain populations, and the need for behavioral change.

But the omission was not limited to HIV. Other sexually transmitted infections—like syphilis, gonorrhea, and HPV—were quietly swept into the shadows of public health discussions. High-risk behaviors and their consequences were reframed or omitted entirely, replaced by generic encouragements for safer sex practices that often failed to address the unique vulnerabilities of specific groups.

Misinformation as a Tool of Cultural Defense

Misinformation also became a weapon, wielded by those who sought to protect their own identities or agendas. In LGBTQ+ advocacy circles, narratives emerged that downplayed the health risks associated with high-risk behaviors, redirecting attention to broader societal challenges like discrimination and legal inequity. While these causes were undeniably important, the selective framing often blurred the lines between addressing stigma and obscuring facts.

"Don't make us the problem," one prominent activist argued in a media interview during the early 2000s. "We've had enough blame. It's time to talk about the systems failing us, not our choices." While the sentiment resonated with many, it inadvertently reinforced a dangerous misconception: that discussing personal behavior equates to victim-blaming. This dynamic fostered an environment where critical discussions about health risks were sidelined.

Media further amplified these narratives, often prioritizing uplifting stories of resilience and progress over uncomfortable truths. Articles celebrating "freedom of choice" and "living authentically" rarely interrogated the tangible costs of risky behavior. The result was a sanitized view of public health— one that ignored the hard realities beneath the surface.

The Cost of Misinformation

Misinformation carries consequences far beyond public perception. In healthcare settings, the lack of honest dialogue about high-risk behaviors contributes to delayed diagnoses, insufficient prevention measures, and poor health outcomes. For women, the cost has been particularly steep.

When heterosexual women contract HIV through partners with undisclosed same-sex relationships, their diagnosis often comes as a double betrayal: first by their partners, and then by a system that failed to equip them with the knowledge to protect themselves. "I didn't know what I was up against," one survivor recounted during an interview for a community health project. "They taught us about condoms and birth control, but no one told us what to look for in a partner. No one told us this could happen."

For men who identify as heterosexual but engage in same-sex behavior, misinformation compounds the problem. Fear of stigma and societal rejection often leads to secrecy, perpetuating cycles of infection and mistrust. The resulting web of lies, omissions, and half-truths ensnares not only the individuals involved but also their families, communities, and partners.

Media's Role in Misogyny

Misinformation about health risks is not the only issue. Media narratives have also contributed to a culture of misogyny within LGBTQ+ spaces. Articles like "The Gay Men Who Hate Women" by *Vice* and *The Advocate*'s exposé on gay misogyny have illuminated how disdain for femininity has permeated queer culture. Terms like "fishy" to describe feminine characteristics on drag shows or casual jokes mocking women's appearances reveal a persistent undercurrent of gendered hostility.

This misogyny is not merely anecdotal; it has real consequences. Women in queer spaces often feel excluded or tokenized, their experiences dismissed as less valid than those of their male counterparts. Meanwhile, women outside these communities bear the brunt of the collateral damage, exposed to health risks and societal pressures while receiving little recognition for their struggles.

To confront the roots of misinformation, society must first reckon with its own discomfort. Addressing the intersection of health risks, cultural narratives, and misogyny requires a willingness to engage with complexity, nuance, and even contradiction. It demands transparency, not just from public health officials but also from advocacy groups, media outlets, and individuals.

The question is not whether society can change—it is whether it is willing to confront the truths that make change possible.

Chapter 3: The Hidden Costs of Misogyny

Summary: This chapter examines the pervasive misogyny found in unexpected places, including LGBTQ+ spaces, and its broader societal consequences. It delves into the subtle and overt ways misogyny manifests, from cultural language to public health outcomes, and highlights its impact on both women and societal cohesion.

The roots of misogyny run deep. For centuries, disdain for women and femininity has shaped societal norms, often hiding in plain sight. In mainstream culture, misogyny is frequently called out and critiqued, yet in some unexpected corners—spaces that pride themselves on inclusivity—it thrives in silence. These are places where it's often dismissed as humor, irony, or an inevitable byproduct of cultural dynamics. But misogyny, wherever it exists, has a cost.

In LGBTQ+ communities, misogyny takes on unique forms, blending societal biases with subcultural dynamics. Gay men, long celebrated for their role in breaking down rigid gender norms, sometimes perpetuate the very attitudes they claim to oppose. Feminine traits, once mocked in straight culture, are often derided as "fishy" or "too much" in queer spaces. Women, even in settings meant to embrace diversity, are left feeling excluded or diminished.

The Feminine Divide

Language is a powerful tool, and in LGBTQ+ spaces, it has often been weaponized against femininity. Phrases like "she's giving fish" or "I can't with her drama" pepper conversations, casually reducing femininity to a punchline. In drag culture, hyper-feminine performances are celebrated on stage but derided off it. The word "fishy," used to describe a queen whose drag appears convincingly female, underscores the tension between admiration and disdain.

This contradiction isn't limited to language. Research has shown that gay men frequently express a preference for masculine traits, both in themselves and their partners. A 2023 study highlighted the pervasive discrimination against feminine-presenting men in gay dating apps. As one respondent noted, "If you don't act straight, you're out." This preference not only marginalizes femininity within gay spaces but also reinforces societal norms that equate masculinity with power and femininity with weakness.

For women, the consequences are palpable. Lesbian and bisexual women in LGBTQ+ spaces often feel tokenized, their experiences overshadowed by the dominant narratives of gay men. In broader society, straight women find themselves grappling with a different manifestation of this misogyny— one that affects their relationships, health, and autonomy.

Collateral Damage in Public Health

The disdain for femininity isn't just cultural; it has real-world implications. Misogyny, whether overt or subtle, contributes to a public health crisis that disproportionately affects women. In heterosexual relationships, women are often left vulnerable to health risks due to the behaviors of their male partners.

When men lead double lives, engaging in same-sex relationships while maintaining a facade of heterosexuality, their female partners often bear the brunt of the consequences. The CDC reports that heterosexual women account for a significant proportion of new HIV diagnoses, often as a result of unprotected sex with partners who do not disclose their sexual history or infidelity with the same sex.

"I never saw it coming," one survivor shared. "We were in love, or so I thought. But he had a whole other life I knew nothing about." Her story is one of many, highlighting the gaps in public health education and the societal stigma that silences open discussions about sexual health.

For women in these situations, the betrayal is twofold. First, there is the personal violation—discovering that a partner has lied about their sexuality or sexual history. Then, there is the institutional failure—a system that has long ignored their unique vulnerabilities and health risks.

Internalized Misogyny

Misogyny within LGBTQ+ spaces is not always directed outward. Many gay men grapple with internalized misogyny, shaped by societal expectations and cultural conditioning. This internal conflict often manifests in their relationships with women, from dismissive language to exclusionary behavior.

For some, this disdain for femininity is a way to distance themselves from the stereotypes of gay culture. By aligning with masculinity, they seek validation in a society that still equates maleness with power. But this alignment comes at a cost, perpetuating the very hierarchies that oppress them.

A Broader Cultural Reflection

The misogyny in LGBTQ+ spaces reflects broader societal norms, where femininity is undervalued and marginalized. In media, politics, and workplaces, women are still fighting for equal representation and respect. The dynamics within queer spaces are a microcosm of this larger struggle, highlighting how deeply ingrained these biases are.

The normalization of misogyny in these spaces also sends a dangerous message: that even in communities built on the principles of inclusion and acceptance, women's experiences are secondary. This double standard undermines the progress made in both feminist and LGBTQ+ movements, creating divisions that weaken their collective power.

Toward Change

Addressing misogyny requires more than acknowledgment; it demands action. LGBTQ+ spaces must confront their biases, challenging the language and behaviors that marginalize femininity. Public health campaigns must prioritize the experiences of women, particularly those affected by the health risks associated with societal stigma and misinformation.

For individuals, the path forward lies in self-reflection and accountability. By examining their own biases and choices, they can contribute to a culture that values and uplifts all expressions of gender and identity.

The cost of ignoring misogyny is too high. It fractures communities, endangers public health, and perpetuates the inequalities that so many have fought to dismantle. But with courage and commitment, it is a cost that can—and must—be overcome.

Chapter 4: The Intersection of Mental Health and Risk

Summary: This chapter explores the role of mental health in shaping behaviors and societal dynamics, focusing on conditions like pica and the psychological roots of risk-taking. It examines how untreated mental illness exacerbates health risks and perpetuates cycles of misinformation, stigma, and harm.

Mental health has long been the silent driver of public health crises, its influence invisible but pervasive. While society often highlights external factors like access to care or economic inequality, it frequently ignores the deeper, psychological underpinnings of behavior. The result is a vicious cycle where untreated mental illness fuels harmful choices, amplifies risks, and perpetuates stigma.

In no place is this clearer than in the realm of public health crises tied to sexual behavior and misinformation. Conditions like pica—a disorder characterized by the consumption of non-food substances—serve as striking examples of how psychological challenges can shape behavior in unexpected and often dangerous ways. Yet, pica is just the beginning of a much larger conversation about mental health and risk.

Pica and the Unseen Links

Pica is frequently associated with mental health conditions such as autism spectrum disorder, schizophrenia, and intellectual disabilities. While its symptoms may seem unrelated to broader societal issues, its underlying cause—a psychological imbalance or untreated mental illness—illustrates the complex interplay between mind and behavior.

Individuals with pica often face stigma and misunderstanding, their behavior dismissed as a curiosity rather than a serious health concern. This same dismissive attitude extends to other risky behaviors, particularly those tied to intimacy and sexual health. Just as society fails to address pica's root causes, it often overlooks the psychological factors driving behaviors that elevate the risk of STIs, HIV, and other public health crises.

Risk-Taking as a Symptom

Psychologists have long studied the link between mental health and risk-taking behavior. For individuals grappling with untreated conditions like depression, anxiety, or trauma, risky behaviors can serve as a form of escape, self-punishment, or even self-validation. These choices are not made in a vacuum—they are shaped by a complex web of personal history, societal pressure, and psychological need.

In LGBTQ+ communities, where stigma and discrimination are still prevalent, mental health challenges are often compounded. The pressures of navigating identity, acceptance, and societal judgment create a fertile ground for untreated trauma. For some, this manifests in behaviors that elevate health risks, from unprotected sex to substance abuse.

The statistics paint a troubling picture. Gay and bisexual men face higher rates of depression and anxiety compared to their heterosexual peers, according to the National Alliance on Mental Illness. Transgender individuals report even higher rates of psychological distress, with nearly 40% considering suicide at some point in their lives. These mental health challenges are not merely personal struggles—they ripple outward, influencing relationships, community dynamics, and public health outcomes.

Misinformation and Mental Health

Misinformation thrives in environments where mental health needs go unmet. For individuals facing untreated conditions, the allure of misinformation lies in its simplicity—it offers explanations, validation, or a sense of control in an otherwise chaotic world. But this reliance on misinformation often exacerbates the very issues it seeks to address.

In public health, misinformation about HIV, STIs, and safe sex practices has had devastating consequences. Myths about transmission, prevention, and treatment persist, fueled by fear, stigma, and a lack of access to accurate information. For those already navigating the challenges of mental illness, these myths can become barriers to seeking care or making informed decisions.

A 2021 study published in *Social Science & Medicine* found that individuals experiencing psychological distress were more likely to believe and share misinformation about COVID-19. This pattern extends to sexual health, where misinformation about HIV and other STIs often reflects deeper anxieties about identity, morality, and self-worth.

The Role of Stigma

Stigma is both a cause and a consequence of untreated mental illness. It prevents individuals from seeking help, perpetuating cycles of harm and isolation. For LGBTQ+ individuals, stigma takes on unique forms, blending societal prejudice with internalized shame. This dual burden not only affects mental health but also shapes behaviors in ways that amplify risk.

Consider the story of David, a pseudonymous figure who spoke candidly in a community health forum. A gay man in his late 20s, David described years of untreated depression and anxiety stemming from his family's rejection of his sexuality. Seeking validation, he turned to risky behaviors, including unprotected sex and substance use. "It wasn't about wanting to hurt myself," he explained. "It was about wanting to feel something—anything."

David's story is far from unique. It reflects a larger pattern of individuals turning to risky behaviors as coping mechanisms for unaddressed mental health needs. Yet, these stories often go untold, overshadowed by narratives that focus solely on external factors like discrimination or access to care.

Breaking the Cycle

Addressing the intersection of mental health and risk requires systemic change. It demands a shift in how society views both mental illness and public health, recognizing the deep connections between the two. Key strategies include:

1. **Expanding Access to Mental Health Care:**
   - Ensure that mental health services are accessible and affordable, particularly for marginalized communities.
   - Train healthcare providers to recognize and address the unique needs of LGBTQ+ individuals.
2. **Combatting Stigma:**
   - Launch public awareness campaigns that normalize seeking help for mental health challenges.

o   Address the specific stigmas faced by LGBTQ+ individuals, women, and other marginalized groups.

3. **Integrating Mental Health into Public Health:**
   o   Treat mental health as a critical component of public health initiatives, particularly those focused on sexual health and STI prevention.
   o   Provide education that links mental health to behaviors, risks, and outcomes.

The Cost of Inaction

The failure to address mental health's role in public health crises carries a heavy cost. It perpetuates cycles of risk, harm, and misinformation, leaving individuals and communities vulnerable. But the potential for change is equally powerful. By recognizing and addressing the psychological roots of risky behaviors, society can break these cycles, creating pathways to better health and greater understanding.

In the end, mental health is not just a personal issue—it is a societal one. Its impact reaches far beyond the individual, shaping the narratives, behaviors, and outcomes that define communities. And only by confronting it head-on can we hope to rewrite the story.

Chapter 5: Public Health and the Price of Silence

Summary: This chapter explores how silence and societal discomfort surrounding health risks and behavioral realities have perpetuated public health crises. It examines the consequences of neglecting transparency, highlights the stories of individuals affected by this silence, and advocates for a culture of open dialogue and accountability.

There is power in silence, but not always the kind that heals. Silence can shield us from discomfort, protect fragile egos, and maintain the veneer of societal harmony. Yet, when silence takes root in public health, it becomes a force of destruction, enabling crises to deepen unchecked. Beneath the surface of health statistics and glossy campaigns lies a world of unspoken truths, where lives are shaped—and too often lost—by what remains unsaid.

The price of silence is steep. It is paid in lives cut short by preventable diseases, in communities fractured by stigma, and in the growing gap between public health narratives and lived realities. To understand the true cost, we must confront the ways in which silence has shaped the public health crises of our time.

The Politics of Silence

Public health is inherently political. The information we choose to highlight—or suppress—reflects societal values and priorities. Over the decades, silence has been used as a tool to navigate contentious issues, particularly those tied to sexuality and gender. The result is a system that often prioritizes comfort over candor, leaving vulnerable populations to fend for themselves.

Take the example of HIV prevention. Early campaigns focused on promoting condom use and safe sex practices, but they often avoided addressing the specific behaviors that carried the highest risks. Discussions about anal sex, for instance, were notably absent from many public health initiatives, even as data consistently identified it as the riskiest form of sexual activity for HIV transmission. This omission was not accidental—it was a calculated choice, driven by a desire to avoid further stigmatizing gay and bisexual men.

While well-intentioned, this silence had unintended consequences. It left individuals without the information they needed to make informed choices and allowed myths about transmission to flourish. Worse, it reinforced a culture of avoidance, where difficult conversations about health risks were sidestepped in favor of vague platitudes.

Women as Collateral Damage

The impact of public health's silence extends beyond those directly targeted by campaigns. Women, in particular, have borne the brunt of this failure. In heterosexual relationships, they are often at the mercy of partners who withhold critical information about their sexual history or health status.

One such story is that of Marcia, a 32-year-old mother of two who contracted HIV from her husband. Unbeknownst to her, he had been engaging in same-sex relationships throughout their marriage. "I trusted him," she said during an interview with a local health organization. "I didn't think I needed to ask questions. Why would I?"

Marcia's story is not unique. The CDC reports that heterosexual women account for nearly 20% of new HIV diagnoses in the United States, many of them contracted through relationships with men who live double lives. These women are often left to navigate the stigma of their diagnosis alone, their stories erased from public health narratives that focus on other demographics.

The Consequences of Avoidance

Silence about health risks doesn't just affect individuals—it undermines entire communities. When critical information is withheld, misinformation fills the void, creating a ripple effect of harm. Misunderstandings about how HIV and other STIs are transmitted fuel stigma, discourage testing, and perpetuate cycles of infection.

For LGBTQ+ communities, silence about health risks has further entrenched internal divides. Misogyny within gay spaces often manifests in dismissive attitudes toward women's health concerns, while the broader public's unwillingness to address high-risk behaviors among men who have sex with men has deepened mistrust between communities. The result is a fragmented public health landscape, where collaboration is replaced by blame and silence by resentment.

Breaking the Silence

Confronting the culture of silence in public health requires a fundamental shift in how we approach difficult topics. Key strategies include:

1. **Normalizing Difficult Conversations:**
   - Public health campaigns must address high-risk behaviors openly and honestly, without fear of stigma or backlash.
   - Discussions about anal sex, same-sex relationships, and other sensitive topics should be included in sexual education curriculums and community outreach programs.
2. **Centering Marginalized Voices:**
   - Women, particularly those affected by the actions of closeted partners, must be included in public health narratives.
   - LGBTQ+ communities should be empowered to lead conversations about their health, ensuring that campaigns reflect lived experiences.

3. **Combating Stigma Through Transparency:**
   - Misinformation thrives in the absence of clear, accurate information. Public health efforts should prioritize transparency, even when the truth is uncomfortable.
4. **Building Trust Through Accountability:**
   - Institutions must take responsibility for past failures, acknowledging the harm caused by silence and committing to more inclusive, honest approaches moving forward.

Stories Worth Hearing

At the heart of these changes lies the need to amplify stories that have long been ignored. Marcia's story, David's struggles with depression, and countless others like them are reminders of the human cost of silence. These stories are not just anecdotes—they are evidence of a system that has failed to meet the needs of its most vulnerable members.

In the words of one health advocate: "Silence is not neutrality. It's complicity. And it's time we stopped paying its price."

A Future Without Silence

Breaking the culture of silence in public health won't be easy, but it is necessary. By confronting uncomfortable truths, amplifying marginalized voices, and fostering open dialogue, society can begin to repair the fractures caused by years of avoidance.

The question is not whether we have the tools to change—it is whether we have the courage to use them.

Chapter 6: Misinformation as a Weapon

Summary: This chapter delves into how misinformation is intentionally and unintentionally wielded to manipulate narratives, obscure accountability, and deflect focus from harmful behaviors. It explores the roles of advocacy, media, and societal norms in perpetuating myths about health risks, behaviors, and public health, highlighting the damaging effects on individuals and communities.

In the age of information, the truth has never been more vulnerable. What should be a time of clarity—where facts are readily accessible—has instead become a battleground where misinformation thrives. It hides in half-truths, cloaked in seemingly well-meaning rhetoric. It masquerades as inclusion, weaponized to protect reputations and deflect accountability. In the public health sphere, misinformation is not just a failure of communication; it is a deliberate tool, used to manipulate narratives and obscure harm.

Nowhere is this more evident than in the discussions surrounding health risks, especially those tied to sexuality, gender, and behavior. While progress has been made in destigmatizing marginalized identities, that progress has sometimes come at the expense of transparency. And when misinformation is wielded as a shield, the fallout is felt by everyone.

The Origins of Misinformation

Misinformation rarely begins as an outright lie. More often, it grows from selective truths—facts presented without context or exaggerated to serve a particular narrative. Advocacy groups, striving to combat discrimination and promote visibility, have sometimes contributed to this problem, albeit unintentionally. In their efforts to protect LGBTQ+ communities from stigma, some have downplayed the health risks associated with high-risk behaviors, focusing instead on systemic injustices.

For instance, discussions about the disproportionately high rates of HIV among gay and bisexual men often frame these statistics as evidence of healthcare inequities. While systemic barriers do play a significant role, this framing sometimes glosses over the behavioral factors that also contribute to these disparities. The result is a narrative that shifts responsibility entirely onto external systems, leaving individuals without the information they need to make informed choices.

But misinformation is not limited to advocacy. Media outlets, eager to promote positive stories of resilience and acceptance, often avoid reporting on the complexities of public health issues. Articles celebrating LGBTQ+ visibility frequently omit discussions of health risks, creating a sanitized view that misleads both individuals and policymakers. This omission is not malicious—it is a reflection of society's discomfort with confronting difficult truths.

Deflecting Accountability

One of the most insidious uses of misinformation is as a tool to deflect accountability. When public health crises emerge, the instinct to shift blame is powerful. Governments blame communities, communities blame systems, and individuals blame societal norms. In the process, the focus shifts away from the behaviors and choices that contribute to these crises, leaving the root causes unaddressed.

This deflection is particularly evident in discussions about STI transmission. While advocacy groups and public health campaigns rightly emphasize the importance of systemic change, they often avoid addressing the role of individual behavior. Conversations about safe sex practices, for instance, are frequently framed in vague terms, avoiding explicit discussions about high-risk activities like anal sex. This reluctance stems from a fear of stigmatizing certain groups, but it ultimately does more harm than good.

Without clear information, individuals are left to navigate their health decisions in a vacuum, relying on incomplete or inaccurate narratives. For women, this dynamic is especially damaging. When health campaigns focus primarily on men, women who contract STIs through heterosexual relationships are often left without the resources or support they need.

Weaponizing Stigma

Misinformation also thrives in the shadows of stigma. Fear of judgment drives individuals to hide their behaviors, creating fertile ground for myths to spread. In communities where stigma around same-sex relationships or nontraditional sexual practices remains strong, misinformation becomes both a shield and a weapon.

One example is the persistent myth that HIV is no longer a significant health concern. Advances in treatment have transformed the virus from a death sentence into a manageable chronic condition, but this progress has led some to underestimate the importance of prevention. Among men who have sex with men (MSM), misinformation about PrEP (pre-exposure prophylaxis) has discouraged its use, despite its proven effectiveness in preventing HIV transmission.

For transgender individuals, misinformation about HIV transmission risks has further compounded existing disparities. Transgender women, who face some of the highest rates of HIV infection globally, often encounter barriers to accurate health information due to societal stigma and inadequate healthcare infrastructure.

The Ripple Effect of Misinformation

The consequences of misinformation extend far beyond individual choices. They shape public policy, influence healthcare funding, and reinforce societal prejudices. When public health campaigns prioritize palatability over accuracy, they fail to address the full scope of the problem. And when misinformation spreads unchecked, it undermines trust in institutions, creating a cycle of skepticism and disengagement.

Consider the case of Marcia, whose story was introduced in Chapter 5. Her husband's failure to disclose his same-sex relationships was rooted in a culture of silence and misinformation. But Marcia's experience was not an isolated incident—it was the product of systemic failures that allowed myths about risk and responsibility to persist.

This ripple effect also impacts LGBTQ+ communities, where internal divides are deepened by misinformation. The misogyny discussed in earlier chapters is reinforced by narratives that dismiss women's health concerns as secondary or irrelevant. Meanwhile, transgender individuals face additional layers of marginalization, their experiences often overshadowed by broader LGBTQ+ issues.

Toward a Culture of Accountability

To combat misinformation, society must embrace a culture of accountability—one that values truth over comfort and transparency over deflection. This requires action on multiple fronts:

1. **Reforming Public Health Campaigns:**
   - Campaigns must prioritize clarity and specificity, addressing high-risk behaviors without fear of stigma or backlash.
   - Education about HIV, STIs, and other health risks should be explicit and evidence-based, avoiding vague or sanitized language.
2. **Challenging Media Narratives:**
   - Media outlets must balance stories of resilience with honest discussions about the challenges facing LGBTQ+ communities.
   - Investigative journalism should shine a light on the systemic and behavioral factors contributing to public health crises.
3. **Empowering Individuals:**
   - Advocacy groups should provide individuals with the tools and information they need to make informed health decisions.
   - Communities must foster open dialogue about health risks, breaking the cycle of silence and stigma.

Misinformation may be a powerful weapon, but it is not invincible. By confronting its roots and exposing its consequences, society can begin to reclaim the narrative. The path forward lies in truth—truth that is uncomfortable, challenging, and necessary.

As one health advocate put it: "We don't need perfect narratives. We need honest ones."

Chapter 7: Misogyny's Lasting Impact

Summary: This chapter explores the long-term effects of misogyny on individuals and communities, particularly in relation to health, relationships, and societal cohesion. It examines how unchecked disdain for femininity perpetuates cycles of harm and exclusion, creating barriers to progress in public health and equality movements.

Misogyny isn't a relic of the past—it's an ever-present force, subtly shaping the dynamics of modern relationships, workplaces, and public discourse. It seeps into spaces that claim to celebrate diversity and inclusion, revealing how deeply ingrained disdain for femininity truly is. For many women, this is not a theoretical problem; it is a lived experience, one that affects their health, safety, and opportunities.

But the most damaging aspect of misogyny isn't always its overt manifestations. It is the quieter, more insidious ways it shapes expectations, narratives, and systems—leaving behind a legacy of harm that goes far beyond the individuals it targets.

Exclusion in LGBTQ+ Spaces

LGBTQ+ spaces are often perceived as havens of inclusivity, yet misogyny within these communities remains a pervasive problem. While gay men have long been at the forefront of LGBTQ+ advocacy, their relationships with women—both within and outside the queer community—are often fraught with tension.

As previously discussed, this tension manifests in casual language, such as the derogatory use of terms like "fishy" to mock femininity. But it also appears in systemic ways, such as the exclusion of lesbian, bisexual, and transgender women from leadership roles within LGBTQ+ organizations. These exclusions send a clear message: women's experiences and voices are secondary, even in spaces designed to challenge patriarchal norms.

For bisexual women, the challenge is even more pronounced. Their identities are frequently erased or invalidated, dismissed as "phases" or subjected to fetishization. Meanwhile, transgender women face both misogyny and transmisogyny, a compounded form of prejudice that leaves them particularly vulnerable to violence and discrimination.

The Health Consequences of Misogyny

Misogyny is not just a cultural issue—it has tangible health implications. Women who contract HIV or other STIs through heterosexual relationships are often overlooked in public health campaigns, which frequently focus on male-to-male transmission. This oversight leaves many women without the resources or support they need, perpetuating cycles of harm.

For instance, heterosexual women account for nearly 20% of new HIV diagnoses in the United States, a statistic that reflects both the risks they face and the systemic failures to protect them. Many of these women are infected by male partners who withhold critical information about their sexual behavior, a betrayal rooted in both stigma and misogyny.

"I was made to feel like it was my fault," one woman shared during a support group meeting. "The doctors told me to use protection, but how was I supposed to know I needed to protect myself from my own husband?" Her story underscores a painful reality: public health systems often fail to address the unique vulnerabilities of women, treating them as secondary to broader health crises.

Misogyny and Power Dynamics

At its core, misogyny is about power. It is the deliberate devaluation of femininity to maintain systems of control, whether in relationships, workplaces, or advocacy movements. These dynamics are not limited to heterosexual spaces; they are equally present in queer communities, where masculinity is often prized over other expressions of gender.

This preference for masculinity reinforces patriarchal norms, even in spaces that claim to challenge them. It creates hierarchies within LGBTQ+ communities, marginalizing those who don't conform to traditional ideas of strength, resilience, or leadership. Women, particularly those who embrace or embody femininity, are often left at the bottom of these hierarchies, their contributions undervalued and their needs ignored.

These dynamics are further complicated by the intersection of race, class, and sexuality. Black and Hispanic women, for instance, face additional layers of discrimination that amplify the effects of misogyny. Their voices are not only excluded but actively silenced, leaving them with few avenues to advocate for their health and well-being.

The Generational Cycle

Misogyny's impact is not confined to the present—it extends across generations. Women who grow up in environments where femininity is devalued often internalize these messages, shaping their relationships, career choices, and self-worth.

This internalized misogyny perpetuates the very systems that harm them, creating a cycle that is difficult to break.

For LGBTQ+ communities, this cycle manifests in subtle ways. Young gay men, exposed to cultural messages that equate femininity with weakness, may distance themselves from women or adopt misogynistic attitudes to align with societal expectations. Meanwhile, young women, particularly those navigating queer identities, may struggle to find spaces that affirm their experiences and perspectives.

The effects of this generational cycle are far-reaching, influencing everything from mental health outcomes to public health initiatives. Without intervention, these dynamics will continue to shape the lives of individuals and communities for decades to come.

Breaking the Legacy

Confronting misogyny requires more than awareness—it demands action. Advocacy groups, public health organizations, and individuals must work together to challenge the attitudes and systems that perpetuate harm. Key steps include:

1. **Amplifying Women's Voices:**
   - Ensure that women, particularly those from marginalized communities, are represented in leadership roles within LGBTQ+ organizations.

- Create platforms for women to share their experiences and advocate for change.
2. **Addressing Misogyny in Public Health:**
   - Develop campaigns that prioritize the health and well-being of women, particularly those affected by STI transmission through heterosexual relationships.
   - Combat stigma by providing clear, accurate information about health risks and prevention strategies.
3. **Fostering Inclusive Spaces:**
   - Challenge exclusionary language and behaviors in LGBTQ+ communities, promoting a culture of respect and inclusion.
   - Support initiatives that celebrate femininity in all its forms, recognizing its value and resilience.

A Path Forward

Misogyny is not an immutable force—it is a learned behavior, shaped by cultural norms and reinforced by systems of power. By confronting its roots and challenging its manifestations, society can begin to dismantle the barriers it creates.

For women, this means reclaiming spaces that have long excluded them and demanding recognition for their contributions. For LGBTQ+ communities, it means embracing the diversity within their ranks, celebrating all expressions of gender and identity. And for public health systems, it means prioritizing the needs of the most vulnerable, ensuring that no one is left behind.

The legacy of misogyny is long and painful, but it is not inevitable. Change is possible—but only if we have the courage to confront the truths we've long ignored.

Chapter 8: Population Trends and Cultural Shifts

Summary: This chapter examines the broader societal implications of population decline in the United States, focusing on how cultural shifts, public health crises, and the marginalization of women intersect to influence demographic trends. It explores the tension between individual choices and collective consequences, challenging readers to consider the role of health, misinformation, and misogyny in shaping the future.

Population trends are not merely numbers on a graph; they are reflections of societal priorities, cultural shifts, and structural inequalities. The decline in birth rates in the United States has become a growing concern, raising questions about the forces driving this change. While economic pressures, delayed parenthood, and changing societal values are often cited as primary causes, there are deeper, less-discussed factors at play—factors rooted in health, misinformation, and the enduring impact of misogyny.

The story of America's population decline is not just about who is choosing to have children—it's also about who is unable to make that choice due to systemic barriers. Women bear the brunt of these challenges, facing a web of health risks, social stigmas, and economic pressures that make parenthood increasingly difficult. At the same time, the broader cultural shifts reshaping gender and identity have introduced new dynamics into the conversation about population trends.

Population Decline in the United States

The United States is no stranger to demographic shifts. In the mid-20th century, the country experienced a post-war baby boom, driven by economic prosperity and traditional family structures. Today, however, birth rates have fallen below replacement levels, with the total fertility rate hovering around 1.6 children per woman—far below the 2.1 needed to sustain population growth.

Unlike developing nations where high fertility rates persist despite limited resources, the U.S. faces a paradox: declining birth rates despite unparalleled access to healthcare, education, and social services. This trend reflects a confluence of factors, from economic instability to shifting cultural norms that prioritize individualism over family life.

But these explanations, while valid, fail to capture the full picture. The health risks disproportionately faced by women, the impact of misinformation on sexual behavior, and the undervaluation of femininity all contribute to a climate where parenthood is increasingly fraught.

Health Risks and Reproductive Challenges

For women, the decision to have children is not just a matter of personal choice—it is deeply influenced by health. Conditions like HIV, which disproportionately affect women in heterosexual relationships, often go unaddressed in public health narratives. These health challenges, compounded by the risks of untreated STIs, can lead to infertility, complications in pregnancy, or the decision to forego parenthood altogether.

One significant barrier is the lack of targeted public health campaigns addressing women's reproductive health. While much attention has been given to male-dominated narratives around HIV prevention, women's needs are often treated as secondary. This neglect creates a ripple effect, leaving many women without the information or resources they need to protect their fertility and make informed choices about their reproductive futures.

"By the time I realized something was wrong, it was too late," shared one woman during a health advocacy panel. Diagnosed with infertility after years of untreated STIs, she spoke of the systemic failures that left her without access to testing, treatment, or education. "It wasn't just my health that was taken—it was my future."

Cultural Shifts and Changing Norms

At the same time, cultural shifts around gender, identity, and relationships have reshaped societal expectations. The growing acceptance of LGBTQ+ relationships, for example, has broadened the definition of family but also introduced new complexities into conversations about reproduction.

Same-sex couples, transgender individuals, and non-binary people all face unique challenges in building families, from legal barriers to limited access to fertility treatments and surrogacy. These challenges highlight the tension between cultural progress and structural inequality, revealing the ways in which systems have failed to adapt to evolving definitions of family.

But these shifts are not without backlash. Traditionalists often point to declining birth rates as evidence of moral decay, blaming LGBTQ+ visibility or women's workforce participation for the perceived erosion of family values. This rhetoric, steeped in misogyny and homophobia, oversimplifies the issue, ignoring the broader economic and social factors driving demographic changes.

The Role of Misinformation

Misinformation also plays a critical role in shaping population trends. Myths about fertility, sexual health, and family planning have led many to make decisions based on incomplete or inaccurate information. For instance, misconceptions about the effectiveness of contraceptives, the risks of certain sexual behaviors, or the accessibility of fertility treatments can discourage individuals from pursuing parenthood.

In LGBTQ+ spaces, misinformation about reproductive options further complicates the issue. Transgender men and non-binary individuals, for example, often face conflicting narratives about their ability to conceive or carry children, creating confusion and anxiety around family planning. Similarly, gay and lesbian couples navigating adoption or surrogacy encounter a maze of misinformation about legal and financial barriers.

This web of misinformation perpetuates cycles of fear, mistrust, and inaction, leaving individuals and communities ill-equipped to navigate the complexities of reproduction and family life.

Economic Pressures and Gender Inequality

Economic instability is another driving force behind declining birth rates, particularly for women. The rising costs of childcare, housing, and education have made parenthood financially prohibitive for many. For single mothers or women in low-income households, these pressures are even more pronounced, creating a significant barrier to family growth.

But economic challenges alone cannot explain the decline. Gender inequality in the workplace continues to limit women's opportunities, forcing many to choose between career advancement and parenthood. The societal expectation that women should shoulder the majority of caregiving responsibilities further exacerbates this divide, discouraging women from pursuing large families—or any family at all.

A Tipping Point

The United States stands at a demographic tipping point. As birth rates continue to decline, the implications for the nation's economy, social fabric, and future stability grow increasingly urgent. Yet, addressing these challenges requires more than policy changes or financial incentives. It demands a fundamental shift in how society values and supports parenthood, health, and gender equality.

Key strategies for addressing population decline include:

1. **Investing in Women's Health:**
   - Expand access to reproductive healthcare and education, ensuring that all women can make informed choices about their health and futures.
2. **Promoting Inclusive Family Policies:**

- ○ Support diverse family structures through legal and financial reforms, including affordable childcare, paid parental leave, and accessible fertility treatments.
3. **Challenging Misinformation:**
   - ○ Launch targeted campaigns to dispel myths about reproduction, fertility, and sexual health, empowering individuals with accurate information.

A New Vision for Growth

Population growth is not just about numbers—it is about creating a society where individuals and families can thrive. This requires more than addressing economic or structural barriers; it demands a cultural shift that values health, inclusion, and equality.

For women, this means reclaiming their role in conversations about health and family. For LGBTQ+ communities, it means ensuring that all individuals have the tools and support they need to build the families they envision. And for society as a whole, it means recognizing that demographic change is not a threat but an opportunity to build a more equitable future.

The question is not whether the United States can reverse its population decline—it is whether it is willing to confront the systems and stigmas that have driven it.

Chapter 9: A Call to Action

Summary: The final chapter ties together the book's key themes—health risks, misinformation, misogyny, and population trends—and provides a roadmap for change. It challenges readers to confront uncomfortable truths, demand accountability, and advocate for systemic reforms that prioritize health, inclusion, and equity.

The time for silence is over.

Throughout history, societies have faced moments of reckoning—times when deeply entrenched norms and practices must be confronted for the collective good. Today, the United States stands at such a crossroads, grappling with the intertwined challenges of public health crises, systemic misogyny, misinformation, and shifting population dynamics. The question is no longer whether these issues exist—it is whether we have the courage to address them.

The threads woven throughout this book reveal a clear picture: silence and misinformation have exacted a steep toll on individuals, families, and communities. Women, particularly, have borne the brunt of these failures, their health, autonomy, and voices too often overlooked. LGBTQ+ individuals, while achieving progress in visibility and rights, remain vulnerable to internal divides and external stigma. And as birth rates decline and public health systems strain under misinformation and inequities, the need for collective action becomes undeniable.

Confronting Health Risks with Transparency

The first step toward change is truth. Public health efforts must prioritize transparency, no matter how uncomfortable the realities may be. The risks of anal sex, the prevalence of HIV and STIs among certain groups, and the behavioral factors contributing to these issues must be addressed openly and directly.

But transparency requires more than just facts—it demands context and compassion. Public health campaigns must frame their messages in ways that empower individuals, rather than shaming or stigmatizing them. Education about sexual health, particularly in schools, must include discussions about high-risk behaviors, LGBTQ+ realities, and the unique challenges faced by women.

Prevention must also go beyond education. Expanding access to tools like PrEP, condoms, and regular STI testing is critical, especially for marginalized communities. Healthcare providers must be trained to deliver care that is inclusive, respectful, and evidence-based, dismantling the barriers of fear and stigma that keep many from seeking help.

Misogyny is a structural problem, deeply embedded in societal norms and institutions. Addressing it requires a multi-pronged approach that tackles its manifestations in language, culture, and policy.

1. **Amplifying Women's Voices:**
   - Women must be at the forefront of conversations about health, policy, and culture. Their experiences, particularly those of women of color and LGBTQ+ women, must be centered in efforts to reform systems that have long excluded them.
2. **Challenging Misogyny in LGBTQ+ Spaces:**
   - Queer communities must confront the misogyny that undermines their claims of inclusivity. This includes holding individuals and institutions accountable for dismissive attitudes toward femininity, supporting women in leadership roles, and fostering a culture of mutual respect.
3. **Reforming Public Policy:**
   - Policies that reinforce gender inequality—such as insufficient parental leave, inadequate childcare support, and pay disparities—must be replaced with reforms that empower women and families.

Misinformation thrives in silence and ignorance. To combat it, society must embrace a culture of critical thinking, where evidence and accountability take precedence over convenience and comfort.

1. **Media Accountability:**
   - Media outlets must be held to higher standards of accuracy, particularly when reporting on public health issues. Stories that sanitize or distort realities in the name of palatability do a disservice to the communities they claim to represent.
2. **Community-Based Education:**
   - Grassroots efforts to educate communities about health risks, reproductive options, and family planning are essential. These initiatives should be led by trusted voices within the communities they serve, ensuring cultural relevance and accessibility.
3. **Digital Literacy:**
   - In an age of social media, teaching individuals to discern credible sources from misinformation is crucial. Public campaigns must equip people with the tools to critically evaluate the information they consume.

Reimagining Population Growth

Declining birth rates in the U.S. present a challenge—but also an opportunity. Rather than lamenting this shift as a crisis, policymakers and communities must view it as a chance to build a more equitable and inclusive society.

1. **Supporting Diverse Families:**
   - Recognize and support nontraditional family structures, including LGBTQ+ families, through legal protections, affordable fertility treatments, and access to adoption services.
2. **Reducing Economic Barriers:**
   - Policies that address the rising costs of childcare, education, and housing will empower families to make choices that align with their goals and values, rather than their financial constraints.
3. **Valuing Parenthood:**
   - Beyond economic support, society must celebrate and value parenthood as a critical contribution to its future. This includes challenging cultural narratives that devalue caregiving and creating workplace environments that support work-life balance.

The Role of Individual Action

While systemic change is essential, individual actions remain a powerful force for progress. Each person has the capacity to challenge misinformation, confront misogyny, and advocate for better health practices within their communities. These small actions, when multiplied, create a ripple effect that can transform societal norms and systems.

A Vision for the Future

The road ahead is not without challenges, but it is also filled with possibility. By embracing truth, prioritizing inclusion, and demanding accountability, society can address the interconnected crises explored in this book. More importantly, it can begin to heal the fractures caused by years of silence, stigma, and neglect.

As the United States grapples with its demographic and cultural shifts, the opportunity to build a more equitable future has never been clearer. This is a chance to redefine what it means to thrive—not just as individuals, but as a collective.

The work begins now.